THE ROSARY:

Mysteries and Testimonies

M A U R E E N   N W A J I O B I

THE ROSARY: MYSTERIES AND TESTIMONIES

iUniverse books may be ordered through booksellers or by contacting:

iUniverse
1663 Liberty Drive
Bloomington, IN 47403
www.iuniverse.com
844-349-9409

Imprimatur: + Daniel Cardinal DiNardo
         Archbishop of Galveston-Houston
         July 26, 2021

ISBN: 978-1-6632-4027-9 (sc)
ISBN: 978-1-6632-4028-6 (e)

Library of Congress Control Number: 2022909557

Print information available on the last page.

iUniverse rev. date: 06/15/2022

To the Daughters of Mary
Mother of Mercy (DMMM)

*

To my family and in loving memory of my dear parents,
Mr. and Mrs. Michael Nwajiobi

CONTENTS

FOREWORD

Most Catholics have prayed the Rosary, either alone or alongside others, at some point in their lives. The widespread use of the Rosary among many Catholics is indicative of its significance in their spiritual lives. The apparition of the Most Blessed Virgin Mary in places such as Lourdes and Fatima have helped to promote awareness of the need to pray the Rosary. Besides, many popes and saints have constantly encouraged the daily recitation of the Rosary among the faithful. Pope St. John Paul II describes the Rosary as his favorite prayer, and St. Padre Pio calls the Rosary "the weapon." In the same vein, the author of this book, who herself prays and values the Rosary and is convinced of its efficacy, seeks to encourage constant praying of the Rosary and deep reflection on its mysteries.

Even though numerous books already have been written about the Rosary, its mysteries are inexhaustible because they are the mysteries of our salvation. This comes across clearly in this book, in which the author, in a very simple, concrete, and insightful manner reflects on the mysteries of the Rosary. It will be difficult to read this book without finding some necessary fruits for your spiritual journey and situation in life. After reading this book, the way you pray the Rosary will never be the same again. You will certainly come to see in a new light many aspects of the mysteries of the Rosary that you probably have taken for granted or have not paid sufficient attention to. Such insights result in a rediscovery of a prayer that you may think that you know very well.

In addition to the author's reflections on the mysteries of the Rosary, the many inspiring stories of the testimonies of the Rosary, which are beautifully presented in the second part of this book and which cut across all spheres of life and situations, all point to one fact: the efficacy of the Rosary. This is a book to be read over and over again.

Fr. Livinus Torty, MSP
Gothenburg, Sweden
November 2020

PREFACE

The Rosary has been an important part of my spirituality since I was a child. Having been born and raised in a Catholic family in which the recitation of the Rosary was a necessary aspect of daily prayers, I have grown up to love and to value this devotion to the Blessed Virgin Mary. Before I entered the religious life, I experienced the efficacy of the Rosary in my own life. Over the years, I have not only known that the Rosary is a powerful and invaluable prayer, but I have also been drawn to reflect deeply on its mysteries, and I have written down some of the insights that I have gained. At different times and in different places, I have met people who have experienced the power of the Rosary and who told me the testimonies of the graces they have received through the praying of this Marian devotion.

I have written this book to use it as medium to share my reflections on the mysteries of the Rosary, as well as the testimonies of those who have experienced miracles of the Rosary. As you read this book, it is my prayer that it will lead you to reflect deeply on the mysteries of the Rosary and to see the Rosary as an invaluable spiritual treasure for your spiritual journey.

It is also my hope that the testimonies of the Rosary that are narrated in this book will inspire in you a greater trust in God and a deeper recognition that Blessed Virgin Mary, the mother of our Lord Jesus, is also your mother, and whenever you pray the Rosary, she intervenes on your behalf and presents your request to her dear son, Jesus Christ, just as she did during the marriage in Cana in Galilee. I pray that you may gain deeper insight into the mysteries of the Rosary and experience the power of the Rosary in your life and tell your own testimonies of graces received through the recitation of the Rosary.

I wish to thank the members of my religious family, the Daughters of Mary Mother of Mercy, for their encouragement and support. I sincerely thank His Eminence Daniel Cardinal DiNardo, who gave the imprimatur. I wish also to express my gratitude to Fr. Livinus Torty, MSP, for writing the foreword, and Fr. Martin J. Lott, OP, for his valuable advice. Lastly, I thank the members of my natural family, the Nwajiobi family, especially my brother, Fr. Michael Jude Nwajiobi, for his support. I remember also my late parents, Mr. and Mrs. Michael Nwajiobi, who taught me to pray the Rosary.

Sr. Maureen Nwajiobi, DMMM
Houston, Texas,
November 2020

INTRODUCTION

This book is about the Rosary, a popular devotional prayer among Catholics around the world and which forms an important part of their everyday spirituality. The book is divided into two parts. The first part consists of short reflections on all the mysteries of the Rosary. The twenty mysteries of the Rosary are presented in such a way as to enable the reader to reflect deeply on these mysteries in order to appreciate God's love and his plan for our salvation in Jesus Christ and also to recognize the special place that God accorded to the Blessed Virgin Mary in his plan for our salvation.

Themes that appear in these reflections on the mysteries of the Rosary include total trust in God, obedience to God's will, faithfulness, patience, holiness, bearing witness, moral courage, and eternal happiness. Through deep reflection on these mysteries, the reader is called to imitate the life and example of Jesus and the virtues of the Blessed Virgin Mary and to pray for the graces necessary to attain eternal salvation.

The second part of this book recounts a number of testimonies regarding graces and miracles received through the praying of the Rosary and the intercession of the Blessed Virgin Mary. The testimonies in this book are drawn principally from stories that people shared with me. Two of these stories, however, are related to my personal experiences.

In certain cases, I have omitted specific sensitive information and details that could reveal the identity of the individuals whose testimonies are shared in this book. These testimonies embrace different aspects of life, such as personal life, spiritual life, married life, and work life, as well as relationships with others. Each testimony shows that no situation that arises in our lives is beyond the reach of God's love and mercy. These testimonies also tell us that the Blessed Virgin Mary intercedes for us. She tells her son Jesus that we have "no wine" and constantly asks us to do what Jesus tells us.

PART 1

THE MYSTERIES OF
THE ROSARY

THE JOYFUL MYSTERIES

The Annunciation

"Hail, favored one! The Lord is with you." But she was greatly troubled at what was said and pondered what sort of greeting this might be. Then the angel said to her, "Do not be afraid, Mary, for you have found favor with God. Behold, you will conceive in your womb and bear a son, and you shall name him Jesus. He will be great and will be called Son of the Most High, and the Lord God will give him the throne of David his father, and he will rule over the house of Jacob forever, and of his kingdom there will be no end." But Mary said to the angel, "How can this be, since I have no relations with a man?" And the angel said to her in reply, "The holy Spirit will come upon you, and the power of the Most High will overshadow you. Therefore, the child to be born will be called holy, the Son of God. And behold, Elizabeth, your relative, has also conceived a son in her old age, and this is the sixth month for her who was called barren; for nothing will be impossible for God." Mary said, "Behold, I am the handmaid of the Lord. May it be done to me according to your word." Then the angel departed from her. (Luke 1:28–38)

In this mystery, we see the angelic salutation and God's message to Mary, given through the angel Gabriel. He announces to Mary that she has found favor with God, and God has chosen her to become the mother of Jesus. The almighty God, the Most High God, did not impose his will on Mary but allowed her to give her consent. When Mary asked how this was to be, as she had not known any man, the angel reassured her that God would realize his plan through the Holy Spirit. The angel informed Mary that her cousin Elizabeth was pregnant in her old age, thereby giving an example of God's power to accomplish the impossible. Mary accepted willingly to be the mother of our Savior.

We are called to emulate Mary's total submission and total abandonment to the will of God. She professed that she is the handmaid of the Lord and longed for the will of God to be done in her life. At times in life, we are tempted to prioritize our own will over God's will. We need to remember that God is almighty; he is our Creator; and he is our life. He knows what is best for us. We therefore must let go of our own will and, like Mary, embrace God's will and plan for us, and trust totally in him.

Our Blessed Mother Mary is highly favored by God by virtue of the merits of Jesus Christ. She brings Jesus to our world, and she brings us to Jesus. Mary is full of grace and can obtain for us all the graces that we need when we ask for her intercession. The holy Rosary is a means for us to obtain graces and favors from God, even in those cases that may seem impossible and hopeless. The assurance that almighty God can do the impossible should encourage us to present our needs to him through the intercession of Mary, the highly favored one.

We pray for the grace to do the will of God at all times and to put our trust totally in him.

The Visitation

> When Elizabeth heard Mary's greeting, the infant
> leaped in her womb, and Elizabeth, filled with the
> holy Spirit, cried out in a loud voice and said, "Most
> blessed are you among women, and blessed is the
> fruit of your womb. And how does this happen to
> me that the mother of my Lord should come to
> me? For at the moment the sound of your greeting
> reached my ears, the infant in my womb leaped for
> joy. Blessed are you who believed that what was
> spoken to you by the Lord would be fulfilled."
> (Luke 1:41–45)

When the angel Gabriel informed the Blessed Virgin Mary
that Elizabeth, her cousin, was pregnant, she believed the words
of the angel and hurriedly went to visit Elizabeth and to spend
time with her and to assist her. The Blessed Virgin Mary showed
an outstanding example of love of neighbor. She did not wait for
Elizabeth to ask for her help; she understood the needs of her cousin
and willingly went to help her. She left behind her own plans and
attended to the needs of another person.

Do we pay attention to the needs of those around us—the
members of our families, our friends, and our work colleagues,
and even the stranger that we encounter? Many times, we focus so
much on our own needs and interests that we fail to see the needs
of our neighbors. Seeing the needs of others is not enough; we must
make efforts to assist others, even if doing so will cause us grave
inconveniences. Do we shy away from the needy, whom God sends
daily on our way, and from the many opportunities that God gives
to us, day by day, to love our neighbors? Let us follow the example of
the Blessed Virgin Mary, who welcomed such opportunities with joy.

Mary does not only bring temporal succor to Elizabeth in her
moment of need, but she also brings to Elizabeth spiritual support.

Mary is highly favored by God and full of grace. Bearing in her womb Jesus, the Son of the Most High God, her greeting fills Elizabeth with the Holy Spirit.

Even the baby in Elizabeth's womb leaped for joy, recognizing the presence of Jesus in Mary's womb. Through the inspiration of the Holy Spirit, Elizabeth acknowledges Mary as the mother of the Lord and proclaims her to be the one who believed the words spoken to her by God.

Our encounters and interactions with others should be an opportunity for them to see Jesus in us—in our words and in our actions. Our lives must have a lasting, positive impact on all those we meet. We have a responsibility to lead them on the path of holiness. For this to be possible, we ourselves must be friends of God and live our lives in union with Jesus and be filled with the Holy Spirit.

We pray for the grace to be attentive to the needs of others and for the courage to assist them, irrespective of what it may cost us. Like Mary, we pray that our lives, our words, and our actions may lead others to recognize the presence of Christ and be filled with the joy and inspiration of the Holy Spirit.

The Nativity of Jesus Christ

The time came for Mary to have her child.

> And she gave birth to her firstborn son. She wrapped him in swaddling clothes and laid him in a manger, because there was no room for them in the inn. Now there were shepherds in that region living in the fields and keeping the night watch over their flock. The angel of the Lord appeared to them, and the glory of the Lord shone around them, and they were struck with great fear. The

angel said to them, "Do not be afraid; for behold,
I proclaim to you good news of great joy that will
be for all the people. For today in the city of David
a savior has been born for you who is Messiah and
Lord. And this will be a sign for you: you will find
an infant wrapped in swaddling clothes and lying
in a manger." And suddenly there was a multitude
of the heavenly host with the angel, praising God
and saying: "Glory to God in the highest and on
earth peace to those on whom his favor rests."
(Luke 2:7–14).

Jesus Christ is born in Bethlehem. God becomes man to save us
from our sins. Jesus Christ, the Son of God, shares in our humanity
to give us a share in his divinity. The nativity of Jesus Christ, as the
angels proclaim to the shepherds, is news of great joy for all the
people. An event already foretold by the prophets, it is joyful news
about God's great love for humanity, a new hope for all creation,
and a new beginning in our relationship with God. It is such a
momentous event that the great multitude of the heavenly host
praise God's majesty and proclaim peace to those on whom God's
favor rests.

We are called to constantly reflect on the mystery of the
incarnation and on the great love that God, our Creator, has shown
us by sending his only begotten Son, Jesus Christ, to the world as our
Redeemer. We see in the nativity of Jesus Christ the unfathomable
love of God. We should therefore be filled with great joy for God's
loving mercy upon us and, together with the angelic host, praise
God for our redemption in Jesus Christ, a mystery that is beyond
our full comprehension.

Indeed, God works in mysterious ways. The Son of God
humbles himself and, in obedience to the Father's will, is born of
the Virgin Mary. He was not born in a palace but in a manger. Our
Savior, Jesus Christ, the king of glory and the prince of peace, chose

5

to be born in a lowly place. From the start, the Savior has identified with the lowly. The news of his birth is not first announced to the rulers and the influential people of the time but to the lowly shepherds keeping watch over their flock at night. At his birth in Bethlehem, together with Mary and Joseph, Jesus Christ shares his first dwelling with the lowly and the disadvantaged.

Born in a manger, Jesus shows us where we can find him. We can find him and see his face in all those who have been offered no place in the inn by society and their friends and families, such as the needy, the poor, the sick, neglected children, and all those children who are not even given the opportunity to see the light of day.

We pray for the grace to be always thankful to God for sending Jesus Christ, his only begotten Son, to the world as our Savior and to see the face of Jesus Christ in the lowly, the needy, and the voiceless.

The Presentation in the Temple

Joseph and Mary went to the temple to present Jesus to the Lord:

> When the days were completed for their purification according to the law of Moses, they took him up to Jerusalem to present him to the Lord, just as it is written in the law of the Lord, "Every male that opens the womb shall be consecrated to the Lord." ... The child's father and mother were amazed at what was said about him; and Simeon blessed them and said to Mary his mother, "Behold, this child is destined for the fall and rise of many in Israel, and to be a sign that will be contradicted (and you yourself a sword will pierce) so that the thoughts of many hearts may be revealed." (Luke 2:22, 33–35)

In the fourth joyful mystery, Joseph and Mary presented Jesus in the temple and accomplished all that they were expected to do, as written in the law of the Lord. In spite of all that they learned about Jesus from the messages they received from the angel of God, the parents of Jesus did not relent in their religious responsibility. They obeyed God's law and presented Jesus in the temple. They were amazed at the things that were said about the child Jesus. The words of Simeon became, for Joseph and Mary, a further confirmation of the revelations about Jesus and his mission, which they had earlier received from God's angel.

Joseph and Mary fulfilled their responsibilities as good and God-fearing parents and presented the infant Jesus to the Lord. It is important that we examine our attitude toward obeying the commandments of God and the precepts of the church. Like Joseph and Mary, do we faithfully and responsibly carry out our religious obligations toward our children and all those whom God has placed under our care? Do we give priority to our religious responsibilities, or are we nonchalant toward them?

During the presentation of the child Jesus in the temple, filled with the Holy Spirit, Simeon, the just and God-fearing man, spoke to Joseph and Mary about the redemptive mission of Jesus, and he told Mary of her place in this mission. Simeon announced to Mary that a sword would pierce her soul. Mary, the mother of Jesus, will be united with her son in his redemptive mission in a special way and also share in his sufferings. This aspect of Mary's role was not directly revealed to her by the angel at the Annunciation. During the presentation in the temple, Mary presented Jesus to the Lord and also offered herself to God to accomplish his divine plan.

Mary said yes to God and accepted participating in God's plan of salvation and to be the mother of the Savior. As God revealed that her role would also entail sharing in the sufferings of Jesus, Mary did not retract the commitments that she had made to the Lord. On the contrary, she trusted in God and offered herself totally to do God's will. Mary stands as a shining example for us to continually trust in God at all times and to offer ourselves totally to him.

We pray for the grace to faithfully and responsibly carry out our religious duties and to offer ourselves to God in purity of heart, that his divine will may be accomplished in our lives.

The Finding of Our Jesus in the Temple

> After three days they found him in the temple, sitting in the midst of the teachers, listening to them and asking them questions, and all who heard him were astounded at his understanding and his answers. When his parents saw him, they were astonished, and his mother said to him, "Son, why have you done this to us? Your father and I have been looking for you with great anxiety." And he said to them, "Why were you looking for me? Did you not know that I must be in my Father's house?" But they did not understand what he said to them. He went down with them and came to Nazareth and was obedient to them; and his mother kept all these things in her heart. (Luke 2:46–51)

In this mystery, we reflect on one of the few incidents in the Bible regarding the hidden years of Jesus. After the celebration of the Passover, Jesus stayed behind in Jerusalem, without his parents knowing that they had gone back to Jerusalem without him. One can only imagine the distress that Joseph and Mary felt when they realized he was missing and during the three days that they looked for Jesus. Mary and Joseph were obviously glad and relieved when they found Jesus in the temple, in the midst of the highly learned, listening to them and asking them questions.

Do we imitate Joseph and Mary, who were worried about the welfare of their child, their loved one, and never relented in their search for him? As challenging as the situation was, Joseph and Mary persevered and trusted in God.

Like the parents of Jesus, we are called to also seek the good and the welfare of our loved ones and neighbors. It will not always be an easy endeavor. Sometimes, we may become anxious, but we must persevere and put our trust in God.

When Mary said to Jesus, "Son, why have you done this to us? Your father and I have been looking for you with great anxiety," Jesus answered, "Why were you looking for me? Did you not know that I must be in my Father's house?" Jesus reminded his parents about his mission on earth. He came to proclaim the good news and to save souls. He stayed back in his father's house, where he belonged.

Although Jesus was filled with zeal for his mission and was eager to ignite the Word of God in the hearts of the teachers in the temple, he went with his parents to Nazareth and was obedient to them. As for Mary, she kept all these things in her heart.

Jesus had a legitimate duty to proclaim the gospel, yet on this occasion, he obeyed his parents and followed them home. He gave us an example of obedience. Do we hold on to our rights and fail to obey legitimate instructions that are given to us by those whom God has placed as our authority? The mother of Jesus teaches us to ponder in our hearts the many things that happen in our lives that we do not fully comprehend and to commit them into the hands of God.

We pray for the grace to seek the good and welfare of others and for the grace of obedience and deep reflection.

THE SORROWFUL MYSTERIES

The Agony in the Garden

> Then going out he went, as was his custom, to
> the Mount of Olives, and the disciples followed
> him. When he arrived at the place, he said to them,
> "Pray that you may not undergo the test." After
> withdrawing about a stone's throw from them and
> kneeling, he prayed, saying, "Father, if you are
> willing, take this cup away from me; still, not my
> will but yours be done." And to strengthen him an
> angel from heaven appeared to him. He was in such
> agony, and he prayed so fervently that his sweat
> became like drops of blood falling on the ground.
> (Luke 22:39–44)

Jesus enters his passion, aware of the suffering and death that
await him, which he had foretold on different occasions. It was a
moment of anguish for Jesus, and he went to the Mount of Olives,
a place where he usually stayed to pray. Jesus withdrew to this place
to pray for the strength to endure his passion. In his agony in the
garden, Jesus prayed steadfastly to God the Father. Mindful of the
many challenges that his disciples would face, Jesus asked them to

pray, so as not to be put to the test. In this way, he showed them the central place of prayer, especially in the most trying moments of life.

How do we react in moments of difficulty? Do we groan and complain, or do we walk on the path of prayer? Do we imitate Jesus, who always prayed and who entered his passion in a spirit of prayer? We are to pray always, especially in the challenging and difficult moments of our lives, and to commit our situations into the hand of God.

Through prayer, we can draw strength from God and experience his abiding presence. Through prayer, we receive God's grace to overcome temptation, for we cannot rely on ourselves or on our own merits.

During the agony in the garden, Jesus expressed his total submission to the Father's will and thus prayed, "Father, if you are willing, take this cup away from me; still, not my will but yours be done." For Jesus, the will of the Father was paramount, and he was committed to doing the Father's will. Jesus had come into the world to do the will of the Father, and he was obedient to the Father and carried out the Father's will faithfully unto the end. Even though the Father's will meant that Jesus would undergo suffering and die on the cross of Calvary, Jesus submitted himself completely to the Father's will.

Jesus gives us a perfect example of what doing God's will is and what it entails. We are called to do the will of God at all times. God, our Creator, loves us so much, and his will is always the best for our lives, even if sometimes we do not seem to fully comprehend it. But are we, like Jesus, ready and willing to do the will of God, irrespective of what it may cost us?

We pray for the grace to pray steadfastly when we face challenges and difficulties in our lives and for the courage to do the will of God at all times, regardless of what it may cost us.

The Scourging at the Pillar

> Then Pilate took Jesus and had him scourged.
> (John 19:1)

Pilate knew that Jesus was innocent and that the chief priests and elders had handed him over out of envy. Pilate, however, was afraid of the crowd and was more concerned about holding on to his position of power and the friendship of Caesar than in giving just judgment or standing for the truth. He handed Jesus to the Roman soldiers to be scourged and crucified.

Our Lord was tied to the pillar and cruelly scourged by the soldiers. He was defenseless. The whips left many bloody scars on his body. We can only imagine the terrible pain that Jesus had to endure as he was scourged. It was an agonizing and sorrowful experience for him.

Our Lord Jesus Christ underwent the scourging at the pillar for our sake. He faced indescribable pain and suffering to save us from sin and death. Neither the pain nor the suffering that he had to endure could deter our Lord from loving us and from dying on the cross for our sins. Neither pain nor suffering should deter us from loving Jesus, who suffered and died that we may have life.

When we consider the terrible suffering that our Lord had to undergo, we might criticize and blame the chief priests and elders, Pilate, and the soldiers for the cruel treatment they meted out to Jesus. Are we really different from these individuals? The truth is that we also contribute, in different ways, to the scourging of our Lord. We contribute to the scourging of Jesus whenever we allow our minds and hearts to be blinded by envy and jealousy. We contribute to the scourging of Jesus every time we choose to protect our own interests, rather than act justly and/or stand for the truth. We also contribute to the scourging of Jesus each time we treat others inhumanly.

In fact, we scourge Jesus at the pillar every time we sin. Do we realize that whenever we sin, we cause our Lord Jesus pain and sorrow? Do we understand that by sinning, we turn our backs on God and on his love? Such a realization should move us to love God, to abhor sin, and to avoid occasions of sin, even if it entails losing the friendship and approval of our fellow human beings.

We pray for the grace to appreciate more deeply the suffering that our Lord Jesus Christ endured for our sake, to love him with all our hearts, and to sincerely repent of our sins.

The Crowning with Thorns

> Weaving a crown out of thorns, they placed it on his head, and a reed in his right hand. And kneeling before him, they mocked him, saying, "Hail, King of the Jews!" They spat upon him and took the reed and kept striking him on the head. (Matthew 27:29–30)

Jesus was scourged at the pillar, and while he was still reeling from the physical pain and the anguish that accompanied it, he was crowned with thorns and subjected to mockery and ridicule by the cruel soldiers. They humiliated him by putting a crown of thorns on his head and a reed in his hand and scornfully hailed him as "King of the Jews." Thus, they made a mockery of the King of kings and Lord of lords. They even further humiliated him by spitting on him, striking him repeatedly on the head, and mockingly asking him to play the prophet by saying who had struck him.

When Jesus suffered humiliation and mockery at the hands of the soldiers, he left an example for us to follow. Our Lord courageously put up with such humiliation and ridicule; he endured it all for love of us and for our salvation. Jesus did not react in anger or threaten anyone. He remained focused on his mission, and his heart was full of love. He was committed to doing the Father's will.

Just as Jesus, our Lord, suffered mockery and humiliation, we also should be ready to face ridicule and humiliation as a result of our Christian faith. Such ridicule and humiliation may come to us in diverse ways and from different sources, such as the state, the media, social institutions, nonbelievers, and even sometimes from our fellow Christians, members of our own families, and our friends.

The mockery and humiliation that we suffer as Christians often discourage us from living out our Christian lives. We may be called names for making efforts to do the right thing, and our core beliefs and religious practices may sometimes be the object of ridicule.

How do we react in the face of the mockery and humiliation that we may suffer on account of our faith? Do we follow Jesus's example? Despite any ridicule and humiliation, we always must remain focused on Jesus, our Lord. The ridicule and humiliation that we encounter will sometimes cause us much pain and sorrow, but we should never harbor anger or hatred for those who ridicule and humiliate us. On the contrary, we are called to show them love and to pray for them. Rather than discourage us, the ridicule and humiliation that we face as a result of our faith should strengthen our resolve to love God and to serve him more and more.

We pray for the grace and the moral courage to stand firm in the face of all veiled and open ridicule and humiliation that we may suffer on account of our Christian faith.

The Carrying of the Cross

> And when they had mocked him, they stripped him of the cloak, dressed him in his own clothes, and led him off to crucify him. As they were going out, they met a Cyrenian named Simon; this man they pressed into service to carry his cross. (Matthew 27:31–32)

Jesus was falsely accused by the chief priests and the elders who wanted to have him killed. He did not receive a just trial; although he was innocent, Pilate handed Jesus over to be crucified. Jesus willingly took his heavy cross and began the agonizing journey to Calvary. He had already suffered much, having been scourged and humiliated by the soldiers, but as he carried his cross and walked along the road, the cruel soldiers continued to mistreat him. He grew increasingly weak under the weight of the heavy cross, having lost much blood, yet he patiently carried his cross—the cross on which he would die to redeem all of humanity.

We are called to carry our crosses and follow Jesus every day. Jesus tells us that "whoever does not carry his own cross and come after me cannot be my disciple" (Luke 14:27). In life, many kinds of crosses come our way. Often, we may have to carry the cross of sickness, accident, death of a loved one, economic hardship, unemployment, disappointment, failure, false accusation, discrimination, insults, or ridicule. In carrying our crosses, we cannot depend on our own strength but on the Lord Jesus. We have to follow in his footsteps, draw strength from him, and imitate his patience.

The soldiers, who were afraid that Jesus might die before reaching Calvary, the place of his crucifixion, forced a passerby, Simon of Cyrene, to help Jesus carry his cross. It was not Simon's intention to carry the cross, and he probably had other plans for that day, but the soldiers compelled him to do so. It was not a situation that the Cyrenian would have loved, but he did his best to assist Jesus. In helping Jesus to carry his cross, Simon must have come to know who Jesus was and to become thankful for his opportunity to assist Jesus on his way to Calvary.

While we have to carry our crosses every day and follow Jesus, we must see the face of Jesus in those who suffer and do our best to help them. We must be ready and willing to help others carry their own crosses. How often do we help others, materially and spiritually, to carry their crosses? Do we make sincere efforts to alleviate the suffering of the others, to encourage and console those who suffer?

Do we wait until we are forced to help others? Do we wait for people to cry for help before we intervene? Do we blame others for their suffering and, in doing so, ignore their needs and add to their sorrows?

We pray for the grace to faithfully carry our crosses and follow Jesus, for patience in times of suffering, and for the courage to do our very best to alleviate the suffering of others.

The Crucifixion

> When they came to the place called the Skull, they
> crucified him and the criminals there, one on his right,
> the other on his left. Then Jesus said, "Father, forgive
> them, they know not what they do." (Luke 23:33–34)

Jesus is crucified. Death by crucifixion was a punishment reserved for the worst offenders during Roman times. This was the punishment that was given to our Lord, even though he was innocent. He was scourged at the pillar, crowned with thorns, ridiculed, beaten on his way to Calvary, and finally, crucified. We can only imagine the indescribable pain that he felt as the nails pierced his hands and feet and as the cross was raised up. He was treated like a criminal and crucified alongside two criminals, one on his right and the other on his left. As he hung on the cross, the soldiers kept making a mockery of our Lord.

Our Lord endured the agony of the cross and persevered to the end. He loved us and gave his life to save us.

> No one has greater love than this, to lay down one's
> life for one's friends. (John 15:13)

By his death on the cross, Jesus transformed the cross into a tree of life. Through his suffering and death, he saved us from sin and death and reconciled us to God.

As Jesus hung on the cross, he taught us forgiveness by his life and his example. He said, "Father, forgive them, they know not what they do" (Luke 23:34). While still in pain and hanging on the cross, our Lord asked his Father to forgive all those who had conspired against him and those who had treated him cruelly. He asked his Father to forgive the chief priests and elders who had falsely accused him and to forgive Pilate, who had sentenced him to death, even though he had committed no crime and was innocent. He prayed for God's forgiveness for the soldiers who had treated him inhumanely. If they had known what they had done, they would have asked for forgiveness.

We are called to imitate Jesus's example of forgiveness. Jesus forgave those who conspired against him and had him crucified, even when they did not ask for forgiveness. Do we have such a forgiving spirit? Do we refuse to forgive our neighbors? If God forgave us in Jesus Christ, should we not forgive others? Forgiveness is a key to a peaceful soul because it releases us from the cage of hatred.

We pray for the grace to continually thank God for the great love and mercy that he has shown to us through his Son, Jesus Christ, who died on the cross to save us from sin and death. We pray also for the grace to forgive those who have offended us and caused us harm.

THE GLORIOUS MYSTERIES

The Resurrection

After the sabbath, as the first day of the week was dawning, Mary Magdalene and the other Mary came to see the tomb. And behold, there was a great earthquake; for an angel of the Lord descended from heaven, approached, rolled back the stone, and sat upon it. His appearance was like lightning and his clothing was white as snow. The guards were shaken with fear of him and became like dead men. Then the angel said to the women in reply, "Do not be afraid! I know that you are seeking Jesus the crucified. He is not here, for he has been raised just as he said. Come and see the place where he lay. Then go quickly and tell his disciples, 'He has been raised from the dead, and he is going before you to Galilee; there you will see him.' Behold, I have told you." Then they went away quickly from the tomb, fearful yet overjoyed, and ran to announce this to his disciples. (Matthew 28:1–8).

Jesus Christ rose from the dead, as he had told the apostles he would. The Resurrection of Jesus Christ is the cornerstone of our faith. St. Paul tells us that if Christ has not been raised from the dead, our faith is vain (1 Corinthians 15:17). Through his Resurrection, Jesus confirmed that he was the Messiah. Through his Resurrection, Jesus won victory over sin and death and opened the gates of heaven for us. We who have been baptized into his death also share in his victory. We are the people of the Resurrection. Death has no power over those of us who believe in Christ. For us, death is not the end of the road but a transition and an entrance into the eternal life of heaven, which God has promised those who love him.

The Resurrection of Jesus Christ from the dead shows us that God always fulfills his promises and that, for him, nothing is impossible. We are to trust all his words and actions. We are called, therefore, to believe God, who raised Jesus from the dead and who has promised us a heavenly inheritance. As we continue on our earthly pilgrimage toward heaven, we are called to trust in God and to depend totally on him in all the challenges that we encounter on our way.

Mary Magdalene and the other Mary made their way at dawn to see the tomb of Jesus on the first day of the week. The death of Jesus had been a painful and sorrowful experience for them, but it did not dampen their love for him. They still wanted to give him all the care and respect that he deserved. Their love for Jesus was rewarded, as they became the first witnesses to the Resurrection of Jesus. The women, "fearful yet overjoyed," quickly ran to announce the Resurrection of Jesus to the disciples, as the angel had told them—a message that was to transform the lives of the disciples and prepare them to encounter the risen Lord.

Like those holy women who were sent to the disciples to announce the news of the Lord's Resurrection, we are all called to constantly proclaim the Resurrection of Jesus Christ and to share with other people the joy of his Resurrection, not only through our words but also through our actions.

We pray, through the intercession of the Blessed Virgin Mary, for strong faith in God and for the grace to always share the joy of the Resurrection with others through our words and actions.

The Ascension

> So, then the Lord Jesus, after he spoke to them, was taken up into heaven and took his seat at the right hand of God. (Mark 16:19)

Jesus completed the mission that the Father had sent him to accomplish on earth. He proclaimed the coming of the kingdom; he suffered, died, and rose from the dead. After his Resurrection, Jesus ascended to heaven to take his place at the right hand of God the Father. Before his ascension, Jesus showed himself to his apostles on different occasions. He told them that all authority in heaven and on earth has been given to him. He promised to be with them to the end of time, and he entrusted to them the mission of proclaiming the gospel and said they were to be his witnesses to the ends of the earth.

The apostles carried out the Lord's commands, and through their witness and that of their successors, we received the gospel. We are called to follow in the footsteps of the apostles—to carry out the Lord's command and to be his witnesses in our days to the ends of the earth. Do we take seriously this mission that has been entrusted to us? What efforts do we make, as a community of believers and as individuals, to bear witness to Christ and to pass on the faith to the next generation?

The ascension of our Lord Jesus Christ gives us the hope of eternal life, for he has gone to prepare a place for us in his Father's house, as he promised he would. Hence, we live our lives here on earth in the hope that where the Lord is, there we also shall be and that we will be united with him when we leave this world. Such hope of union with God and of eternal life comforts and strengthens us in the midst of the many sorrows, trials, and sufferings that we have to go through in the course of our earthly lives. It constantly reminds us that life on earth is transient and that "our citizenship is in heaven" (Philippians 3:20).

As we live our lives here on earth and as we carry out the mission that our Lord has entrusted to us, we are called to always hold on to the hope of eternal life and to "seek what is above, where Christ is seated at the right hand of God" (Colossians 3:1). Amid the toils and the distractions of life, do we rely on the grace of God and constantly desire and expect eternal life?

We pray that through the intercession of our Blessed Mother Mary, we may bear witness to the Lord and be filled with hope for eternal happiness, which God has promised those who love him and do his will.

The Descent of the Holy Spirit

> When the time for Pentecost was fulfilled, they were all in one place together. And suddenly there came from the sky a noise like a strong driving wind, and it filled the entire house in which they were. Then there appeared to them tongues as of fire, which parted and came to rest on each one of them. And they were all filled with the holy Spirit and began to speak in different tongues, as the Spirit enabled them to proclaim. (Acts 2:1–4)

Before Jesus ascended to heaven, he told his apostles to remain in Jerusalem until they received power from on high. He promised them that the advocate, the Holy Spirit, whom the Father would send in his name, would enlighten them regarding all that he had taught them.

Faithful to the command of Jesus, the apostles remained in Jerusalem, and together with the mother of Jesus and other followers of Jesus, they devoted themselves to prayer. On the day of Pentecost, the promise that Jesus made to them was fulfilled. They were filled with the Holy Spirit as they were all gathered in one place. The Holy Spirit manifested its presence in forms of a strong, driving wind and tongues of fire that rested on each of them.

Since the birthday of the church on the day of Pentecost and through the ages, God has continued to fill his church with the Holy Spirit. Like the disciples of Jesus, we ourselves have received the Holy Spirit; we received the Holy Spirit at baptism and confirmation. Are we cognizant of the great gift that we have received? Are we thankful to God for filling us with the Holy Spirit through these sacraments of the church?

Filled with the Holy Spirit, the disciples of Jesus began to speak in different tongues. The Holy Spirit transformed and empowered them. All who encountered the disciples were astounded at the transformation that had taken place in their lives. Many who had come to Jerusalem from different parts of the then-known world were amazed to hear the disciples speak in their own native languages.

When the Holy Spirit descended on the disciples, he filled them with the power and courage to proclaim the gospel without fear. They were no longer afraid of the local religious authorities and were willing to obey God rather than men. Even when they were punished and humiliated on account of their faith, they rejoiced for having been found worthy to suffer for the sake of the name of Jesus. Filled with the Holy Spirit, they were willing and ready to die for the gospel.

The disciples opened their hearts to the Holy Spirit, and they were transformed by his power. As we have received the Holy Spirit through baptism and confirmation, we should not resist his gifts and his promptings; we should open our hearts to him. Through the Holy Spirit, God will transform and empower us and remove from our hearts every form of fear that inhibits us from living out our lives as his adopted children.

We pray for a greater openness to the Holy Spirit and to his gifts so that we may be led by him and experience his transforming power in our lives.

The Assumption of the Blessed Virgin Mary

> A great sign appeared in the sky, a woman clothed with the sun, with the moon under her feet, and on her head a crown of twelve stars. ... When the dragon [the rebellious angel, the devil] saw that it had been thrown down to the earth, it pursued the woman who had given birth to the male child. But the woman was given the two wings of the great eagle so that she could fly to her place in the desert, where, far from the serpent, she was taken care of. (Revelation 12:1, 13–14)

In this mystery, we reflect on the Assumption of the Blessed Virgin Mary. The Assumption of Mary, the mother of Jesus, is not explicitly recorded in sacred scripture, but belief in it has always been part of the tradition of the Catholic Church. The Assumption of the Blessed Virgin Mary was solemnly defined as a divinely revealed dogma on November 1, 1950, by Pope Pius XII. The church teaches us:

> The Most Blessed Virgin Mary, when the course of her earthly life was completed, was taken up body and soul into the glory of heaven. (Catechism of the Catholic Church 1994, no. 974)

The Assumption of the Blessed Virgin marked the completion of her earthly mission.

God accorded the Blessed Virgin Mary an important role in the mystery of our salvation. The Blessed Virgin Mary shared intimately in the life and ministry of Jesus, her son. God prepared her for this role and "from the first moment of her conception, by a singular grace and privilege of almighty God and by virtue of the merits of Jesus Christ, savior of the human race, preserved her immune from all stain of original sin" (Catechism of the Catholic Church 1994, no. 491).

She found favor with God, and she is blessed among all women. Having been taken up to heaven, body and soul, at the end of her earthly life, the Blessed Virgin Mary shares in the glory of Jesus, her son, in heaven.

The Blessed Virgin Mary represents for us a shining example and a perfect model of humility and obedience to God's will. She carried out faithfully the earthly mission to which God entrusted her as the mother of the Savior, and she is now united with Jesus Christ her son and shares in his glory in heaven. If we imitate the example of the Blessed Virgin Mary, trusting in God at all times and faithfully doing his will in all things, we also will share in the glory of Jesus, her son, in heaven.

As we reflect on the Assumption of the Blessed Virgin Mary, we are reminded that heaven is our true homeland. As we live our lives here on earth, we are called to always keep this in mind and to see heaven as our final goal.

We pray for the grace of a happy death so that at the end of our earthly lives, we may share, together with the Blessed Virgin Mary, in the glory of Jesus Christ in heaven.

The Coronation of the Blessed Virgin Mary

A great sign appeared in the sky, a woman clothed with the sun, with the moon under her feet, and on her head a crown of twelve stars. She was with child and wailed aloud in pain as she labored to

> give birth. Then another sign appeared in the sky;
> it was a huge red dragon, with seven heads and ten
> horns, and on its heads were seven diadems. She
> gave birth to a son, a male child, destined to rule
> all the nations with an iron rod. (Revelation 12:1–5)

In the fifth glorious mystery of the Rosary, we reflect on the coronation of the Blessed Virgin Mary as queen of heaven and earth. Like the fourth glorious mystery, the Assumption, the coronation of the Blessed Virgin Mary is a Catholic tradition that is not recorded explicitly in the Bible. The queenship of the Blessed Virgin Mary is celebrated on August 22, a week after the celebration of the Assumption. In the litany of Loreto (or the litany of the Blessed Virgin Mary, as it is also called), the queenship of the Blessed Virgin Mary is expressed in diverse ways such as Queen of Angels, Queen of Patriarchs, Queen of Prophets, Queen of Apostles, Queen of Martyrs, Queen of Confessors, Queen of Virgins, Queen of All Saints, Queen of Families, and Queen of Peace.

The Second Vatican Council teaches us that Mary "has been exalted by the Lord as queen of all, in order that she might be more fully conformed to her Son the Lord of lords and the conqueror of sin and death" (*Lumen Gentium* 1964, no. 59). The queenship of Mary helps us to recognize the special role and place that God accorded her in the mystery of salvation. God gave her graces in a measure that no other human being has or will ever receive.

The queenship of Mary does not undermine our worship of God. On the contrary, it enhances our worship of God as we acclaim and proclaim the great things that God has done for her by virtue of the merits of Jesus Christ.

The Blessed Virgin Mary is a queen who never forgets her children. She does the will of God, and she wants us to do the same. She shares in the glory of her son in heaven, and she wants us to share in that glory. After her Assumption, she has continued to assist us from heaven. She constantly intercedes for us before God. The

Queen of Heaven never ceases to assist us on our earthly pilgrimage and to lead us to her son, Jesus Christ.

In her apparitions in places such as Lourdes and Fatima, she shows her concern for our salvation. Through her messages, which emphasize prayer and repentance, and through the miraculous cures that occur in these places of her apparition, she gives us the necessary help we need to come closer to God and to yearn for eternal life.

We pray for greater devotion to the Blessed Virgin Mary, the Queen of Heaven and earth. Let us place ourselves under her patronage and make her the queen of our lives and ask her to intercede for us before God.

THE LUMINOUS MYSTERIES

The Baptism of Our Lord

> Then Jesus came from Galilee to John at the Jordan
> to be baptized by him. John tried to prevent him,
> saying, "I need to be baptized by you, and yet you
> are coming to me?" Jesus said to him in reply,
> "Allow it now, for thus it is fitting for us to fulfill
> all righteousness." Then he allowed him. After
> Jesus was baptized, he came up from the water
> and behold, the heavens were opened for him, and
> he saw the Spirit of God descending like a dove
> and coming upon him. And a voice came from
> the heavens, saying, "This is my beloved Son, with
> whom I am well pleased." (Matthew 3:13–16)

In this mystery, our Savior allowed himself to be baptized
by John the Baptist in the Jordan River. Although Jesus, the Son
of God, was sinless, he came to John to be baptized. John the
Baptist, who had recognized Jesus and leaped for joy in his mother's
(Elizabeth's) womb, once again recognized him. Knowing who
Jesus was, John hesitated because Jesus was the spotless Lamb of
God and had no need of baptism. Though John had been baptizing

others, he acknowledged that he was indeed the one who needed to be baptized by Jesus. Jesus, however, insisted that John baptize him because he wanted to fulfill all righteousness. John finally obliged and baptized Jesus.

Jesus is the beloved Son of God. He humbled himself and became man to accomplish the will of the Father. He was like us in all things but sin. By willingly submitting himself to be baptized, Jesus showed solidarity with humanity, in that he had come to redeem us from sin, and he taught humility through his words and actions.

We also see such humility in the life and words of John the Baptist, who acknowledged how unworthy he was to baptize Jesus. Are we humble in our relationship with God and with our fellow human beings?

Even though our Savior, Jesus Christ, did not need baptism, his baptism in the Jordan marked the beginning of his public ministry. When Jesus stepped out of the water after his baptism, the heavens were opened, the Spirit of God descended on him like a dove, and the voice of the Father was heard from heaven, confirming that Jesus was his beloved Son with whom he was well pleased, the one he sent to redeem the world.

Before his ascension into heaven, Jesus commissioned his disciples to "make disciples of all nations, baptizing them in the name of the Father, and of the Son, and of the Holy Spirit" (Matthew 28:19).

We are called to reflect on our baptisms and on our lives as baptized Christians. On the day of our baptisms, we were reborn of water and the Holy Spirit and became adopted children of God, children of the light, and heirs of the kingdom. Are we faithful to our baptismal promises? Do we live our lives as the beloved children of God, with whom God, our Father, is well pleased?

We pray for humility of heart and for the grace to be ever conscious of our Christian identities and to be faithful to our baptismal promises.

The Wedding at Cana

> When the wedding hosts ran out of wine, the mother of Jesus said to him, "They have no wine." And Jesus said to her, "Woman, how does your concern affect me? My hour has not yet come." His mother said to the servers, "Do whatever he tells you." Now there were six stone water jars there for Jewish ceremonial washings, each holding twenty to thirty gallons. Jesus told them, "Fill the jars with water." So, they filled them to the brim. Then he told them, "Draw some out now and take it to the headwaiter." So, they took it. (John 2:3–8)

Mary, the mother of Jesus, was present at the wedding in Cana, and Jesus and his disciples also were invited. In the course of the ceremony, the wedding hosts ran out of wine. Obviously, things had not gone as the hosts had planned. They were suddenly faced with an uncomfortable and embarrassing situation. Our Blessed Mother Mary noticed the challenge that the wedding hosts faced. She presented the situation to Jesus and simply said to him, "They have no wine." Mary knew what Jesus could accomplish and completely trusted him to come to the aid of the wedding hosts and to save them from embarrassment.

When we invite Blessed Mother Mary to our hearts and homes, she will come with her son, Jesus. She is our loving mother, and she easily perceives the challenges and problems that we face. She will present them to her son and ask him to come to our assistance. This is exactly what she did for the wedding hosts at Cana. Jesus granted his mother's request, even when his "hour has not yet come." He would not refuse the requests the Blessed Mother made on our behalf.

The events at the wedding at Cana reveal to us Mary's deep knowledge and trust in Jesus; she trusted and believed that her request would be granted. When Jesus said to her, "Woman, how does your concern affect me? My hour has not yet come," Mary knew that Jesus would assist the wedding hosts, and that was why she said to the servants to do whatever Jesus told them.

The servants listened to both Mary and Jesus. They did not question the seemingly ridiculous instructions that Jesus gave them; rather, they carried out these instructions faithfully. They filled the jars to the brim, and they witnessed a miracle. Jesus turned water into wine, and the wine was the best of all.

Our Blessed Mother is full of grace, and she knows, understands, loves, and trusts Jesus much more than any other human being does. When we pray the Rosary, we are asking our Blessed Mother to intercede for us. She presents our prayers and petitions to Jesus, knowing that her loving son will help us. But Mary does not only bring our requests and needs to Jesus; she also brings us closer to him and asks us every day to carry out, trustingly and lovingly, whatever Jesus tells us.

We pray that the Virgin Mary may intercede for us in our various needs and in the many challenges that we face in life and bring us ever closer to Jesus, her son.

The Proclamation of the Kingdom

> Blessed are the poor in spirit, for theirs is the kingdom of heaven. ... Blessed are they who hunger and thirst for righteousness, for they will be satisfied. (Matthew 5:3, 6)

In this mystery, we are presented with Jesus's proclamation of the kingdom. In the Sermon on the Mount, at the beginning of Jesus's public ministry, he taught his disciples, "Blessed are the poor in spirit, for theirs is the kingdom of heaven" (Matthew 5:3). He taught the disciples, right from the onset, about the importance of total reliance on God.

We all are helpless without the saving grace of God. In our helplessness, God, in his love, sent Jesus Christ, his only begotten

Son, to the world to save us from sin and death and to teach us what we have to do to enter the kingdom of heaven.

It is necessary to be poor in spirit in order to enter the kingdom of heaven. This means an acknowledgment of our nothingness, our sinfulness, and our need for God. It is in such a spirit of humility that we can truly show contrition for our sins and open our hearts to God and to the transformative power of his grace. For the poor in spirit, there is no place for pride or arrogance because without God, we can do nothing. Do we constantly recognize our need for God and his grace?

A recognition of our need for God involves a yearning for righteousness and holiness, a burning desire to do God's will. Jesus proclaimed, "Blessed are they who hunger and thirst for righteousness, for they will be satisfied" (Matthew 5:6). God is holy. As Christians, we are called to holiness. It is God's will that we hunger and thirst for righteousness and holiness. God gives us the grace that we need to live a life of holiness, a life that is pleasing to him, and a life that is worthy of our Christian calling. Our Lord Jesus Christ has promised us that those who hunger and thirst for righteousness will be satisfied.

We are called to holiness, and it is important that we thirst and hunger for righteousness every day, throughout our lives. The call to holiness is therefore a call to grow deeper and continually in God's grace, as long we are alive here on earth. Do we yearn for righteousness and holiness? Does our way of life inspire others to be poor in spirit and to hunger and thirst for righteousness?

We pray that through the intercession of our Blessed Mother Mary, we may continually realize our need for God and constantly yearn for holiness.

The Transfiguration

> After six days Jesus took Peter, James, and John
> his brother, and led them up a high mountain by

> themselves. And he was transfigured before them; his face shone like the sun and his clothes became white as light. And behold, Moses and Elijah appeared to them, conversing with him. Then Peter said to Jesus in reply, "Lord, it is good that we are here. If you wish, I will make three tents here, one for you, one for Moses, and one for Elijah." While he was still speaking, behold, a bright cloud cast a shadow over them, then from the cloud came a voice that said, "This is my beloved Son, with whom I am well pleased; listen to him." (Matthew 17:1–5)

In this mystery, Jesus revealed his glory to the three disciples, Peter, James, and John. He took these disciples to the mountain and allowed them to see his glory, the glory of the Son of God. Jesus wanted to strengthen them in their faith and to prepare them for the challenges that awaited them in the future, starting with his coming suffering and death on the cross. Jesus wanted the disciples to realize that he would enter into his glory through suffering and death. The presence of Moses and Elijah during the transfiguration was a confirmation that Jesus was the Messiah and of all that he had taught his disciples.

When Jesus told the disciples that he would suffer greatly, be killed, and be raised on the third day, it was difficult for his disciples to understand. It was not what they expected to happen to the Messiah. Jesus did not want the apostles to lose heart. He wanted them to know that what was important was not their own views and expectations of the Messiah but God's own plan for the Messiah. We are called to open our hearts to the plan and will of God, rather than hold on to our own views and expectations.

The transfiguration was a wonderful and overwhelming experience for the disciples. When Peter, James, and John witnessed and saw a glimpse of Jesus's glory, they did not want the experience to end. For them, it was a foretaste of heavenly glory, an experience that was greater than any human experience and one that could not be compared or quantified in human or earthly terms. The disciples wanted to remain on the mountain and continue to behold the glory of the Son of God. Hence, it was not surprising that Peter asked Jesus if he could make three tents on the mountain—one for Jesus, one for Moses, and one for Elijah.

God gives us occasional glimpses of eternal glory throughout our lives, such as the fervor we feel in prayer and through the many wonderful things that he does in our lives. These experiences should be life-transforming events that help us to realize that God wants us to behold his glory at the end of our lives. Do we strive every day of our lives to remain in God's love so that we may witness his everlasting glory? If we want to share in eternal glory, we must listen to Jesus.

We pray for the grace to always be open to God's plan, to listen to Jesus, and to yearn for eternal glory that God has promised to those who love him.

The Institution of the Eucharist

> Then he took the bread, said the blessing, broke it, and gave it to them, saying, "This is my body, which will be given for you; do this in memory of me." And likewise, the cup after they had eaten, saying, "This cup is the new covenant in my blood, which will be shed for you." (Luke 22:19–20)

The Eucharist is our Lord's gift of love to his church. Jesus gave us this great gift of his body and blood, and he has promised that whoever eats his body and drinks his blood will never die but will have eternal life. Before his death on the cross, our Lord instituted the Eucharist during the Last Supper with the apostles and commanded them to celebrate it in memory of him. He gave them the power to celebrate the holy Mass and to consecrate the bread into his body and the wine into his blood. Since the institution of the Eucharist, the church has faithfully carried out the Lord's command throughout the ages.

What gift could be greater and more precious than this great gift of love that we have received from the Lord—his abiding presence among us in the Eucharist? Do we really appreciate the magnitude of the boundless love that God has shown us through this great gift? We are called to be eternally thankful to God for the gift of love—the body and blood of Christ that has been given to us.

The Eucharist is a sign of our union with Jesus Christ and a sign of his love for us. Our Lord ascended into heaven but continues to remain with us through his Eucharistic presence. The Eucharist unites us in the love of Christ and gives us a share of his divine nature. It strengthens the life of grace within us, and it gives us the grace to do God's will, to live for Jesus, and to live a life that's worthy of our Christian calling. In addition, the Eucharist nourishes us and forms us more and more into the image of Christ and ignites within us a yearning to have a share in his glory in heaven.

In the Eucharist, we receive the spiritual nourishment we need on our journey to heaven. How do we respond to this great gift of love and to this invitation to be united with Jesus and to grow in grace? Do we avail ourselves of the opportunities that we have been offered? Do we attend Mass regularly and participate actively in the Eucharistic celebration? Do we receive Holy Communion? Do we make time to adore Jesus in the blessed sacrament where he is always present and waiting for us?

We pray for the grace to be always thankful for the great gift of love—the body and blood of Christ—and that we may be formed more and more into the image of Christ, whose body and blood we receive so that we may have a share in his glory in heaven.

PART 2

ROSARY TESTIMONIES

PRAYING FOR PREGNANCY

There was a certain young woman called Anna who got married to the love of her life. The first few years of their married life were blissful, but as time went on, it became clear that all was not well. Anna had yet to conceive after five years of marriage. Together with her husband, she visited several specialist doctors and underwent a series of medical tests. These tests yielded negative results, and it was difficult for the doctors to determine the reason for her inability to conceive.

Like her husband, Anna became very worried, and she cried every night. Her husband tried his best to console her, but her husband's family became increasingly impatient with her for not bearing a child after five years of marriage. The social pressure originating from her husband's family was very difficult for Anna to handle, and it took a heavy toll on her emotional well-being, leaving her depressed.

One day, her friend at the workplace where they served as waitresses noticed her worried look and gloomy appearance, and she asked Anna what was troubling her.

With great hesitancy and sadness in her heart, Anna shared with her friend the distress she had been experiencing because of her inability to conceive a child. Anna sobbed as she related her story.

Anna's friend listened to her story, comforted her, and suggested that she visit the grotto of the Blessed Virgin Mary in the local church to ask for her intercession.

A few days later, Anna went to the grotto of Blessed Virgin Mary and cried out her heart in prayer, asking the Virgin Mary to assist her in her need. When she went home that day, she felt peace and relief, and she prayed the Rosary steadfastly, asking the Blessed Virgin Mary to intercede for her before God.

The following year, Anna conceived and later gave birth to triplets (two boys and a girl). For Anna, she conceived and gave birth to triplets through the intercession of the Blessed Virgin Mary.

A CHANGE OF PERSPECTIVE

Gertrude and Mark met at the university in their early twenties. Both of them were very active in the Catholic chaplaincy at the university. They got married a few years later and planned to have a big family.

They had four young daughters and earnestly wanted to have at least one baby boy. In their efforts to have a baby boy, God blessed them with an additional two baby girls. Initially, the situation was difficult for both Gertrude and Mark to accept, for they really wanted to have a male child.

On one occasion when Gertrude and Mark were praying the Rosary together with their young children, Gertrude felt inspired to consider their longing for a male child from a different perspective, instead of brooding unnecessarily over the matter. She shared this perspective with Mark, who warmly welcomed the idea.

Consequently, rather than continue to pray for a male child, Gertrude and Mark decided to ask the Blessed Virgin Mary to obtain for them the grace to be continually grateful to God for the gift of their six daughters and to help them to raise their daughters in the fear of God and to provide for them a sound education. This marked a turning point in their married life.

Today, both Gertrude and Mark are in their late sixties, and whenever they look back at their life together, they continue to express their gratitude for the graces that the Blessed Virgin Mary obtained for them. All their six children grew up to become responsible and learned adults. Their "six girls," as Gertrude and Mark still prefer to refer to their daughters, are not only their pride and joy, but they are also a source of inspiration to their various families.

Gertrude and Mark are also delighted that their daughters are actively serving their local parishes and communities in different capacities. Gertrude and Mark are deeply convinced that their recitation of the Rosary was instrumental in helping them to have a needed change of perspective—to discover the will of God for their lives and the readiness to accept it with joy.

IN SEARCH OF A LIFE PARTNER

Cecelia was brought up in a Catholic family. She was her parents' first child, and she had one brother and two sisters. She took her Catholic faith very seriously and often went to Mass not only on Sundays but also during the week.

Cecelia has a well-paid job in the telecommunications sector, where she has worked for more than eleven years. Despite being comfortable materially, she has not been so lucky in her love life. It has been very difficult for Cecelia to find the right man—a man who genuinely loves her. She has had three relationships with men at different times in the past. None of these ended well because these men only wanted to exploit her for their own benefit, while claiming to love her.

These past experiences left their mark on Cecelia. They broke her heart and made her mistrustful of men who came close to her. Sometimes, she wondered whether the failure of her past relationships was not indeed her own fault. When her two younger sisters got married, although she shared in their joy, her anxiety concerning her own future only got worse. Her parents intervened and encouraged her not to be worried, but she could see in their facial expressions how worried they themselves had become because of her situation.

On her thirty-eighth birthday, Cecelia resolved to pray more about her situation and to commit her growing anxieties and hopes regarding her future into the hands of the Blessed Virgin Mary. Cecelia decided also to participate more actively in the Legion of Mary in her local parish. She had been a member of the association for many years. It was through her active participation in this group that Cecelia met John, an ardent devotee of the Blessed Virgin Mary.

John was very mature, prayerful, eloquent, caring, and good-humored, qualities that Cecelia had always prayed for the man of her dreams to possess. Cecelia and John became close, fell in love, and married two years later on Cecelia's fortieth birthday. The couple are now blessed with two children.

SEEKING EMPLOYMENT

❈

A woman had an only son who had been trying unsuccessfully to secure a job after graduating from college. Although her son had good grades in college, he had not gotten the type of job that he wanted. The woman became worried about her son's inability to get a job, whereas his friends from college were already working. The challenge of trying to get the right job obviously led the young man to become frustrated and depressed.

Even though the woman was a Catholic and attended Mass regularly, and she knew about the power of praying the Rosary, she was not a devotee of the Blessed Virgin Mary.

One day when she went for Mass, she felt inspired to pray the Rosary for the intentions of her son. When she began to pray and to ask the Blessed Virgin Mary to help her son to get a job, nothing seemed to happen.

Some invitations for job interviews arrived, and her son attended all of them, but no job offers were made to him. At this point, the woman was tempted to give up, but she persevered and continued to pray the Rosary for several months, asking for the intercession of the Virgin Mary for her son to secure a job.

One day, her son was invited for a job interview at a new IT company in a neighboring city. He had applied for a position in the company many months earlier and had forgotten all about it, as he had neither received acknowledgment of his application nor been invited for a job interview. As the young man set out for the interview, his mother prayed and touched a big picture frame of the Blessed Virgin Mary, imploring her to answer her prayer.

Later in the day, her son called to announce the good news—he had been successful in the interview and had been offered a job. What was surprising was that he was offered a higher position than the one for which he had applied.

The woman was filled with great joy and expressed gratitude to God for intervening in the case of her son through the intercession of the Blessed Virgin Mary.

FREED FROM THE TORMENTS OF EVIL SPIRITS

A young man was constantly tormented by evil spirits in his dreams. He had countless nightmares in which evil spirits kept threatening to harm him or to make him harm other people. When he first began to have these nightmares, he tried to ignore them and did not give them any special attention or thought. As time went on, however, he could no longer disregard these nightmares and the threats that evil spirits repeatedly made to him in his dreams. These nightmares deprived him of a good night's sleep, making him tired and unwell during the day, especially at work. This adversely affected his work output.

He also noticed that the threats that the evil spirits made to him in his dreams were having an increasingly negative impact on his mental and emotional well-being. He had become more anxious and was overly worried when it was time to go to bed. He was scared to be alone in the dark and had to leave his lights on all night long.

Initially, he thought that he could handle the situation on his own, but he eventually had to admit that he could not. Although he was born and raised Catholic, he had not practiced the faith for many years. He began to pray for God's help and decided to schedule a meeting with the priest at the local parish.

The priest was very kind to him, counseled him spiritually, and prayed for him. The priest also blessed a rosary and gave it to him, instructing him to pray it daily and to wear it constantly around his neck. When he got home that evening, he prayed the Rosary and wore it around his neck that night.

That same night, he had the worst nightmare of all, with the angry evil spirits threatening to cause him grievous harm if he did not stop wearing the rosary around his neck. When he woke up the next morning, the young man resolved to wear the rosary at all times and to pray the Rosary daily.

Even though he was wearing the rosary and praying it daily, he still had a few dreadful nightmares. Gradually, however, the nightmares lessened and finally stopped. The man's mental and emotional well-being improved significantly, and his spiritual life was revived. He thanked our Blessed Virgin Mary for rescuing his life through the Rosary. Most importantly, he is no longer afraid of darkness, and he now sleeps well at night.

GRACE OF HUMILITY

Job had a good Catholic upbringing, and as an adult, he made an effort to practice his faith to the best of his ability. He went to Mass regularly, prayed a lot, and also tried to assist those in need in the parish community and in his neighborhood. Job participated actively in many activities in the parish.

For the people in the local parish, Job was a devout man and an ideal parishioner. Many parishioners often commended him for all his efforts and contributions in the church. Job felt very happy whenever people commended him for his good works in the parish.

His pride, however, gradually began to take hold of Job. He felt sad and angry whenever his opinions were not accepted by others in the parish and when people did not take notice or commend him for the things he did in the church. He believed that he was better and more knowledgeable than other people and that most people in the parish were not doing enough to support the parish.

On different occasions, he accused people of being selfish, of not praying enough, and of living unspiritual lives. As time went on, Job became increasingly arrogant and angry, and this led him into conflict with some members of the parish, including the parish priest and the members of the Parish Council, whom he criticized time and again. His changing behavior baffled not only those parishioners who had known him for a long time but also the members of his own family.

The priest invited Job for a dialogue and advised him to tone down his condemnation of others in the parish community, but Job was unflinching in his resolve to have things done in his own way— "the right way."

Annette, Job's wife, discussed and argued with him several times regarding his attitude toward people in the parish. Job did not accept that he had done anything wrong. Annette made it a point of duty to pray the Rosary daily, asking the Blessed Virgin Mary to obtain for Job the grace of humility.

After a few months, Job realized his mistakes and acknowledged that he had become consumed by self-righteousness and pride without even realizing it. Thereafter, he became so humble and reconciled with the priest and other people in the parish.

Today, Job constantly prays for the grace of humility for himself and for others.

SAVED FROM A TOXIC WORK ENVIRONMENT

Mark was an intelligent and a gifted young man who secured employment in a pharmaceutical company. Right from his first day at work, he felt that his coworkers were unfriendly toward him. It seemed as if he was not welcome in the workplace. He noticed that whenever he asked his colleagues questions, some of them were unwilling to provide answers, and they were not keen to assist him when he needed help from them. He ignored their behavior and worked very hard to discharge his assigned duties to the best of his ability, but he was never given any positive feedback or commendation. Instead, his mistakes were often emphasized and blown out of proportion. This made Mark very sad and discouraged. He prayed the Rosary regularly and asked for God's help to overcome the challenges that he was facing in his workplace.

After his first year of working in the company, Mark made suggestions to his colleagues on ways to enhance efficiency and innovation in their work. Some of the workers were not positively disposed to his suggestions; they wanted no changes and preferred that things remain as they were. Mark was obliged to withdraw his suggestions when he sensed anger and aggression from his colleagues, many of whom felt threatened by his presence in the company.

They became increasingly unfriendly in their attitude toward Mark and conspired to make false accusations against him so that his employment could be terminated. They accused Mark of being unsuitable for his current position in the company, of being unfriendly, and of never accepting criticism. Mark's employer did not want to fire Mark initially, but the employees who made false allegations against Mark were friendly with the employer and came from the same country as the employer. They pressed the employer to fire Mark "for the good of all."

As the pressure intensified, the employer caved in and fired Mark. One cold, windy morning, as Mark arrived for work, the employer summoned him to his office and informed Mark that his employment was terminated, effective immediately. Mark could not believe his ears. His heart sank, and he felt some rumblings in his stomach. He could barely drive home. It was hard for him to understand how God and Blessed Virgin Mary could allow this to happen to him. But he refused to give in to his anger and sense of disappointment. He cried and prayed to God and recited the Rosary, asking God to come to his aid through the intercession of Blessed Virgin Mary.

Mark was out of work for about eight months, but he later secured a better job in a very friendly and supportive work environment. He was very happy in his new job and even thanked God for allowing him to lose his former job at the pharmaceutical company.

QUIT SMOKING AND DRINKING

Peter had a very difficult childhood. When he was thirteen years old, Peter lost his parents and elder sister on the same day in a ghastly automobile accident. They were the people who mattered most in his life. The sudden death of his parents and his sister shattered him and caused him enormous pain. He had been very close to his mother, and the thought of never seeing her again was a pain too much to bear. He felt sad and alone.

Peter went to live with his aunt, his mother's younger sister. Although his aunt and her family did their very best to make him feel happy and welcome in their family, Peter could not be happy. The love that his new adopted family showed him could never compare to the love his parents and elder sister had shown him. He missed them so much and thought about them often.

In school, he was frustrated and distracted, and he increasingly lost interest in his studies. Sometimes, he just sat in class and gazed, oblivious to the things happening around him. His school reports became very bad, and the school guidance counselor asked to meet with him on several occasions.

Some years later, when he turned eighteen, Peter began to smoke and drink. Three years later, he went for rehabilitation and managed to stop smoking and drinking but only for a short while. He was unemployed and continued to depend on his aunt for support.

His aunt made honest efforts to assist Peter to quit smoking and drinking but to no avail. She did not want to be strict with Peter because of the sad tragedy he had experienced as a child. She was convinced that Peter was a good person who had been adversely affected by personal tragedy.

She prayed for Peter and encouraged Peter to pray the Rosary and to ask for the intercession of the Blessed Virgin Mary. At the beginning, Peter did not show any special interest in praying the Rosary, but he soon started to join her and her family in their daily recitation of the Rosary.

After a long struggle, Peter finally quit smoking and drinking. Now, he is currently working as a truck driver. For Peter, through the recitation of the Rosary, he received the grace to stop smoking and drinking, and God gave him a new life, a job, peace, and happiness, for which he previously had searched in the wrong way.

A TRANSFORMED LIFE

Emmanuel was born into a Catholic family. The family attended the holy Mass every Sunday and prayed daily at their home. Even though Emmanuel joined his family in their daily prayers, he did so reluctantly and was easily distracted in the course of the prayers.

He was a strong-willed and obstinate child who always wanted to do things his own way, and he often refused to obey his parents' instructions for him. He quarreled and fought regularly with his sibling and friends in school. Like at home, he disrespected his teacher at school and bullied younger children.

His life changed when his parents encouraged him and insisted that he join other children in attending a Rosary prayer group (Rosary group) in the neighborhood.

The first day he attended the prayers, he became captivated by a beautifully framed picture of the Blessed Virgin Mary and the three children at Fatima, and he gazed at it continuously for a long time. In addition, he was fascinated by the sense of devotion and seriousness that the other children exhibited as they prayed the Rosary together. He became very interested in the group and wanted to participate more and more in the prayers.

The more he attended the prayers and prayed the Rosary with other children, the more there was a change in his attitude and behavior. His relationship with his parents, siblings, teachers, and schoolmates improved tremendously. These individuals were surprised at the transformation that was taking place in Emmanuel's life.

Today, Emmanuel is an adult and staunch devotee of the Blessed Virgin Mary. He attends the holy Mass regularly and propagates the recitation of holy Rosary among young people and adults alike.

When Emmanuel speaks of his experiences now, he says that something deep and inexplicable happened to him on the day he gazed at the picture of the Blessed Virgin Mary and prayed the Rosary with other neighborhood children. Emmanuel continually expresses his gratitude to his parents, who encouraged him to join other children in praying the Rosary. He is also grateful to God for the many graces that he has received through the intercession of the Blessed Virgin Mary.

FACING UNUSUAL OCCURRENCES

A young Catholic couple and their three children moved into a new apartment in a suburb of a major city. The people who had rented the apartment previously had lived in it for little more than a month. They had left hurriedly, complaining of certain unnatural occurrences in the apartment.

The owner of the apartment could not comprehend what was happening, but he had difficulty getting people to rent the apartment and was worried that he was losing rental income. He decided to cut the rent for the apartment to make it more attractive.

The cheap rent caught the attention of the young couple, who had recently moved to the city. Although people living in the neighborhood were aware of the unusual events associated with the apartment, no one informed the couple of the prevailing state of affairs.

As the young couple and their children moved into the apartment, their neighbors expected them to flee from the house just as former tenants had. These neighbors were surprised to observe that the new occupants of the apartment did not abandon their home and appeared to be happy and comfortable living in it.

As years passed and the couple and their children continued to live in the apartment, one of their curious neighbors informed the couple of the strange experiences of the former occupants of the apartment and how they had all left in a hurry. The neighbor wondered how they had managed to continue living in the apartment.

The couple informed the curious neighbor that when they had moved in, they experienced a lot of strange happenings in the house, such as strange and frightful sounds at night and unexplained movement of objects in the house. The couple acknowledged that they and their children were initially frightened because of these abnormal occurrences, but they committed themselves to the daily recitation of the Rosary and asking for God's protection through the intercession of the Blessed Virgin and for serenity and tranquility to be restored to the apartment.

After a short time, the unexplained happenings in the apartment finally ceased. The curious neighbor was so moved by their story that although she was not Catholic, she asked the couple to give her a rosary and to teach her how to pray it.

A MOMENT OF
EXTERNAL GRACE

Prisca and Angela were roommates at the university. Both of them came from Catholic homes, but whereas Prisca was a devoted Catholic, Angela was but a nominal Catholic and cared very little about religion. Angela rarely prayed and had been away from the sacraments for a very long time.

Prisca prayed every day and talked regularly about her Catholic faith, but Angela showed no interest in such discussions and complained often that Prisca prayed too much. On occasion, she even described Prisca as a hypocrite. At times when Prisca greeted or spoke to Angela, Angela would ignore her completely.

Whenever Prisca invited Angela to go with her to Mass, Angela angrily rejected the invitation and mocked Prisca. Angela humiliated Prisca in many other ways as well. Prisca felt angry on such occasions but decided to endure the mockery and humiliation, and she prayed ardently, asking the Blessed Mother of God to obtain for her the grace to forgive Angela and to show her love despite her actions. Prisca also prayed regularly for Angela.

On a certain day when Prisca came back from Mass, she greeted Angela, and to Prisca's amazement, Angela responded warmly to her greeting and stared at Prisca for a long time. Prisca wondered why Angela kept staring at her.

Almost in tears and in a voice filled with remorse, Angela asked Prisca to forgive her for being mean and unfair to her while they had been living together. Angela said that she was moved by the fact that despite her humiliating and mocking Prisca, Prisca had continued to act with maturity and to show her love. Angela was moved to kneel down as she asked for Prisca's forgiveness.

Prisca told Angela that she had been praying for her and had asked for the intercession of the Blessed Virgin Mary for the grace to forgive her and to show her love.

Angela began to join Prisca in praying the Rosary, and she gradually began to attend Mass and returned to the sacrament. For Angela, living with Prisca became a moment of external grace.

OVERWHELMED BY GOD'S GRACE

Kenneth attended a Catholic college for boys. At the college, there was a well-behaved group of three boys who excelled in their studies. These boys had been raised by devout Catholic parents who taught them to show respect for others, to work hard, and to say their prayers regularly, especially the Rosary. These boys sometimes prayed the Rosary together during their recess time and encouraged other students to join them. Many students admired them, and teachers at the college encouraged other students to emulate the exemplary conduct of the three boys.

The attention and commendation accorded the three students often made Kenneth angry. As a matter of fact, Kenneth would have loved to be like the three boys, but he was not humble enough to join their group. He was often envious of the three boys, and instead of imitating their good behavior, Kenneth began to plan for their downfall. He devised plans to get them in trouble and to damage their reputation.

One hot afternoon during school recess, the three boys assembled other boys and began to pray the Rosary with them. On his way from the restroom, Kenneth heard the boys praying in a classroom. Seeing them, he felt it was an opportunity to put his plans into action. He intended to enter the classroom and disrupt their prayers to provoke the boys into a shouting match.

When he entered the classroom and saw the boys devoutly reciting the Rosary, however, he was overcome by the prayers. Before he realized it, he had knelt down and began to pray with them. He could not explain what happened to him, but instantly, he felt drawn and overpowered by the grace of God. He could not carry out his earlier plans as he had intended; in fact, he renounced his plans and from that day forward, he began to join the three boys in praying the Rosary during school recess.

This incident transformed Kenneth's life. He became tremendously on fire with great love and devotion to the Blessed Virgin Mary. Today, Kenneth is a priest in a religious order. He has continued to be a devotee of the Blessed Virgin Mary.

SAVED FROM LIFE ON THE STREETS

Christiana had a difficult childhood and upbringing. Her parents were very poor and could not take proper care of her. Her father, a day laborer, died after a long sickness when Christiana was barely sixteen years old. The family spent most of their resources during the father's illness.

Following the death of her father, life became even more difficult for Christiana and her mother, who could no longer provide for their basic needs. Christiana quit school, left home, and went to live in a faraway city, cutting off communication with her mother. She looked for work for many months but was unsuccessful in her search. The little money she had was depleted, and she could not get help from anyone.

Unable to pay her rent, Christiana became homeless and lived on the streets, which marked a very dark period in her life. She began to keep bad company, and she took drugs and engaged in begging and occasionally in prostitution. On one occasion she was arrested for shoplifting but was later released. One day, when Christiana was begging on the street, a passerby gave her some money and a little rosary kit that contained a rose-colored rosary and a leaflet on how to say the Rosary. Christiana kept the rosary kit in her bag; she even forgot about it for a while. After some weeks, however, her mind kept going to that rosary kit. As a child, she had prayed the Rosary sometimes with her mother.

One day when she was totally weighed down and almost ready to give up on life, Christiana took out the rosary kit, read the accompanying leaflet, and decided to pray the Rosary for the first time in many years. As she prayed the Rosary, she began to see herself in a new light. It was as if a veil that covered her eyes had been removed. She cried. She regretted her actions and asked for God's forgiveness. As she continued to pray the Rosary, it became clear to her that she could not continue to live on the street. Christiana decided to return home to live with her mother.

Although life has not been fully easy for her and her mother since she came home, Christiana remains very thankful to God for giving her the grace to return to God, returning home, saving her from the streets, and securing a job that sustains her family.

HEALED OF MENTAL ILLNESS

A certain young man had a severe mental illness. He was so aggressive that he had to be restrained most of the time. People stayed away from him, fearful of his aggressive nature. One day, I was passing by at the pilgrimage center where he had been confined in chains for a long time. The man called me, "Sister, Sister."

At that time, I had not entered the religious life, but I realized he was referring to me, and so I turned to him.

Pointing at my neck, he said to me, "Sister, please could you give me your rosary?"

I was surprised because I knew that my clothing covered my rosary, and it was impossible for him to have seen it. I asked him, "To which rosary are you referring?"

He pointed at my neck again.

I touched my neck to check if he could indeed see my rosary. When I realized that he could not see the rosary because it was under my clothing, I asked him again, "To which rosary are you referring?"

He pointed once more at my neck and said, "That black rosary."

I became afraid yet surprised. I wondered how he knew that I was wearing a black rosary. I realized that there was more to it and that it was extraordinary. I asked him, on an impulse, "Will you be healed if I give you the rosary?"

"Yes," he answered with confidence.

I slowly brought out the rosary, gave it to him, and left.

I attended morning mass the next day, and during the intercessory prayer, a familiar voice started reading out one of the prayers, and I turned to take a look. To my bewilderment, it was the man to whom I had given my rosary the day before. I was astonished to see him and equally astonished that he was no longer in chains. He appeared to have been healed the moment he received the rosary.

I marveled all through the Mass. After the Mass, I ran after him and spoke with him. He told me about himself and said that he had wanted to become a priest but had abandoned his seminary studies and relocated to Lagos, one of Nigeria's busiest cities. Eventually, he had become mentally ill, and his friends and relatives took him to the pilgrimage center for healing. I believe that God used the Rosary to heal the man.

SAVED FROM A GUNSHOT

The last testimony that I would like to relate took place when I was writing this book. In my natural family, we have a family WhatsApp platform, through which we communicate, pray, and share inspirational materials to encourage one another in the faith. Over time, we began to pray the holy Rosary and organized a twenty-four-hour Rosary prayer chain, in which each member of the family was expected to pick at least an hour-long prayer slot for the recitation of the twenty decades of the holy Rosary.

At the beginning, we had the twenty-four-hour Rosary prayer chain weekly, but later, we decided to have it on the first Saturday of every month. All the members of my family who participated in the twenty-four-hour Rosary chain prayer were very happy and fulfilled to take part in it. For them, it was a source of blessing in their lives.

The twenty-four-hour Rosary prayer chain was of great interest to my niece, a young woman in her early twenties who was studying to become a registered nurse. Her enthusiasm for the prayer was always evident in her voice each time I spoke with her about it. Not long ago, on the Feast of St. Joseph the Worker, my niece went to a shop across the road from her residence in the company of her younger sister. While they were in the shop, she brought out her mobile phone to show something to her sister. Suddenly, a young man came into the shop, grabbed her phone, and took off.

Initially, she thought that it was a prank, played on her by one of her brother's friends, so she ran after the young man to ask him to give back her phone. She did not realize that the young man was armed with a gun. As she approached him, he turned abruptly, shot her repeatedly at close range, and fled the scene.

She fell to the ground and soon after was rushed to a nearby hospital. She was operated on, and a total of seventeen bullets were removed from her leg. Although she suffered severe injuries, she recovered. My niece credits her survival to the intercession, motherly protection, and intervention of the Blessed Virgin Mary.

CONCLUSION

This book has been about the Rosary, its mysteries, and the testimonies of people who have prayed it. The mysteries of the Rosary are the mysteries of our salvation. This book encourages a deep reflection on the Rosary to help us to appreciate, in a more profound way, God's love for us, our salvation in Jesus Christ, and the place of our Blessed Mother in God's plan.

In this book, the mysteries of the Rosary are presented in such a way as to help us to imitate the life and example of our Savior, Jesus Christ, and the virtues of the Blessed Virgin Mary. It emphasizes reflection on the mysteries of the Rosary that leads us to total trust in God, love of God and neighbor, and obedience to God's will. It encourages us to embrace a life of holiness, humility, faithfulness, kindness, patience, witnessing to the faith, moral courage, and walking on the path of eternal salvation.

The numerous testimonies of miracles that people have experienced in praying the Rosary, which are described in this book, inspire faith, and teach us about God's love. These testimonies also show us that the Blessed Virgin Mary is always ready to come to our aid and to intercede for us, as she did at the wedding at Cana, when the wedding hosts ran out of wine. Through her intervention, her son Jesus Christ performed his first miracle. The Blessed Virgin

Mary is full of grace, and she continues to intercede before her son for all those who call upon her.

Your life will never be the same again if you make the time to pray the Rosary faithfully and to reflect deeply on its mysteries, as this book proposes. You will be drawn into a closer union with God, and you will also have many personal testimonies to give about praying the Rosary.

The spiritual insights that you have gained in reading this book are not meant for you alone. They are to be shared with others, your family members, friends, and members of your parish. In sharing your own experiences with others, you will not only lead them to discover the mysteries of the Rosary and to have testimonies of their own, but you will also deepen your faith and your experience of the mysteries and testimonies of the Rosary.

REFERENCES

Catholic Church. *Catechism of the Catholic Church.* Vatican City: Libreria Editrice Vaticana, 1994.

Second Vatican Council. *Dogmatic Constitution on the Church: Lumen Gentium.* Solemnly promulgated by His Holiness Pope Paul VI on November 21, 1964. Accessed April 6, 2020. https://www.vatican. va/archive/hist_councils/ii_vatican_council/documents/vat-ii_const_19641121_lumen-gentium_en.html.

The Litany of Loreto—Litany of the Blessed Virgin Mary. Accessed January 17, 2022. https://www.vatican.va/special/rosary/documents/litanie-lauretane_en.html.

United States Conference of Catholic Bishops. "How to Recite the Rosary." Accessed January 17, 2022. https://www.usccb.org/how-to-pray-the-rosary.

United States Conference of Catholic Bishops. Accessed January 17, 2022. "Prayer to St. Joseph after the Rosary." https://www.usccb.org/prayers/prayer-st-joseph-after-rosary.

APPENDIX

How to Recite the Rosary

1. Make the Sign of the Cross.
2. Holding the Crucifix, say the *Apostles' Creed*.
3. On the first bead, say an *Our Father*.
4. Say one *Hail Mary* on each of the next three beads.
5. Say the *Glory Be*.

6. For each of the five decades, announce the Mystery (perhaps followed by a brief reading from Scripture) then say the *Our Father.*

7. While fingering each of the ten beads of the decade, next say ten Hail Marys while meditating on the Mystery. Then say a *Glory Be.*

    (After finishing each decade, some say the following prayer requested by the Blessed Virgin Mary at Fatima: *O my Jesus, forgive us our sins, save us from the fires of hell; lead all souls to Heaven, especially those who have most need of your mercy.)*

8. After saying the five decades, say the *Hail, Holy Queen,* followed by this dialogue and prayer:

    V. Pray for us, O holy Mother of God.

    R. That we may be made worthy of the promises of Christ.

    Let us pray: O God, whose Only Begotten Son, by his life, Death, and Resurrection, has purchased for us the rewards of eternal life, grant, we beseech thee, that while meditating on these mysteries of the most holy Rosary of the Blessed Virgin Mary, we may imitate what they contain and obtain what they promise, through the same Christ our Lord. Amen.

    (How to Recite the Rosary, https://www.usccb.org/how-to-pray-the-rosary.)

You may say the prayer to St. Joseph.

Prayer to Saint Joseph

To you, O blessed Joseph, do we come in our tribulation, and having implored the help of your most holy Spouse, we confidently invoke your patronage also.

Through that charity which bound you to the Immaculate Virgin Mother of God and through the paternal love with which you embraced the Child Jesus, we humbly beg you graciously to regard the inheritance which Jesus Christ has purchased by his Blood, and with your power and strength to aid us in our necessities. O most watchful guardian of the Holy Family, defend the chosen children of Jesus Christ; O most loving father, ward off from us every contagion of error and corrupting influence; O our most mighty protector, be kind to us and from heaven assist us in our struggle with the power of darkness.

As once you rescued the Child Jesus from deadly peril, so now protect God's Holy Church from the snares of the enemy and from all adversity; shield, too, each one of us by your constant protection, so that, supported by your example and your aid, we may be able to live piously, to die in holiness, and to obtain eternal happiness in heaven.

Amen.

(Prayer to Saint Joseph, https://www.usccb.org/prayers/ prayer-st-joseph-after-rosary.)

Conclude the Rosary with the Sign of the Cross, now or after the recitation of the Litany of the Blessed Virgin Mary.

The Litany of Loreto (Litany of the Blessed Virgin)
Lord, have mercy.
Christ, have mercy.
Lord, have mercy.
Christ, hear us.
Christ, graciously hear us.
God, the Father of heaven,
have mercy on us.
God the Son, Redeemer of the world,

God the Holy Spirit,
Holy Trinity, one God,
Holy Mary,
pray for us.
Holy Mother of God,
Holy Virgin of virgins,
Mother of Christ,
Mother of the Church,
Mother of Mercy,
Mother of divine grace,
Mother of Hope,
Mother most pure,
Mother most chaste,
Mother inviolate,
Mother undefiled,
Mother most amiable,
Mother admirable,
Mother of good counsel,
Mother of our Creator,
Mother of our Saviour,
Virgin most prudent,
Virgin most venerable,
Virgin most renowned,
Virgin most powerful,
Virgin most merciful,
Virgin most faithful,
Mirror of justice,
Seat of wisdom,
Cause of our joy,
Spiritual vessel,
Vessel of honour,
Singular vessel of devotion,
Mystical rose,
Tower of David,

Tower of ivory,
House of gold,
Ark of the covenant,
Gate of heaven,
Morning star,
Health of the sick,
Refuge of sinners,
Solace of Migrants,
Comfort of the afflicted,
Help of Christians,
Queen of Angels,
Queen of Patriarchs,
Queen of Prophets,
Queen of Apostles,
Queen of Martyrs,
Queen of Confessors,
Queen of Virgins,
Queen of all Saints,
Queen conceived without original sin,
Queen assumed into heaven,
Queen of the most holy Rosary,
Queen of families,
Queen of peace.
Lamb of God, who takes away the sins of the world,
spare us, O Lord.
Lamb of God, who takes away the sins of the world,
graciously hear us, O Lord.
Lamb of God, who takes away the sins of the world,
have mercy on us.
Pray for us, O holy Mother of God.
That we may be made worthy of the promises of Christ.
Let us pray.

Grant, we beseech thee, O Lord God, that we, your servants, may enjoy perpetual health of mind and body; and by the glorious intercession of the Blessed Mary, ever Virgin, may be delivered from present sorrow, and obtain eternal joy. Through Christ our Lord.

Amen

(The Litany of Loreto—Litany of the Blessed Virgin Mary. https://www.vatican.va/special/rosary/documents/litanie-lauretane_en.html.)

Printed in the United States
by Baker & Taylor Publisher Services